The Epic of Cader Idris

The Epic of Cader Idris

(or how not to lose yourself in the hills)

SAMATAR ELMI

BLOOMSBURY POETRY
LONDON · OXFORD · NEW YORK · NEW DELHI · SYDNEY

BLOOSMBURY POETRY
Bloomsbury Publishing Plc
50 Bedford Square, London, WC1B 3DP, UK
29 Earlsfort Terrace, Dublin 2, Ireland

BLOOMSBURY, BLOOMSBURY POETRY and the Diana logo
are trademarks of Bloomsbury Publishing Plc

First published in 2024 in Great Britain by flipped eye publishing
This work is published by Bloomsbury Publishing Plc
by arrangement with flipped eye publishing

This edition published 2024

Copyright © Samatar Elmi, 2024

Samatar Elmi is identified as the author of this work in accordance
with the Copyright, Designs and Patents Act 1988.

All rights reserved. No part of this publication may be reproduced or
transmitted in any form or by any means, electronic or mechanical,
including photocopying, recording, or any information storage
or retrieval system, without prior permission in writing
from the publishers

A catalogue record for this book is available from the British Library

ISBN: PB: 978-1-5266-7520-0;
eBook: 978-1-5266-7581-1; ePDF: 978-1-526675828

2 4 6 8 10 9 7 5 3 1

Typeset by Laura Jones-Rivera
Printed and bound in Great Britain by
CPI Group (UK) Ltd, Croydon CR0 4YY

To find out more about our authors and books
visit www.bloomsbury.com and sign up for our newsletters

Author's Note

Variant spellings of Cader/Cadair Idris are used throughout the book to honour the necessary slippages of language over time.

Contents

Tie as Leash	1
In Conversation with Sarod	2
We Played Some Open Chords	3
Looking for Flowers in Winter	4
The Epic of Cader Idris Playlist	5
The Snail	8
[Etymologies]	9
The Pen	12
Portrait of Colossus as an Immigrant	13
The Invaders	14
The N Word	15
Step This Way	16
Turtle Neck	17
Hargeisa	18
Seed	19
Shield	21
Goole Station	23
The Gallows	26
The Mug	27
Quasimodo and Esmeralda	28
Layla and Majnun	29
Kaleidoscope (i)	30
Requiem	31
Broken Biscuits	32
Marbles	34

The Hammock	35
حرية	36
Daffodils and Daisies	41
Glissando	42
空気を読む	43
The Universe Formerly Known as God	44
Orpheus as a Busker	45
The Game	46
Orisons	47
Brenin Llwyd	49
On the End of the World	50
The End of History	52
A Darker Light	53
Slipstream	54
Coda	55
The Algoriddim	57
Do You Have Your Dunny Documents for Armageddon?	58
A Pale Blue Flower	59
The Epic of Cadair Idris (Rhizomatic Meditations)	61
Where the Colour Blue Was Made	76
Kaleidoscope (ii) (36mg)	77
How I Learned to Fight	78
England	79
Ohms	80
Lighthouse	82
Die Welt	84
Only Foals and Horses	86
The Kite	87

Poets utter great and wise things which they do not themselves understand.

    – Plato

It is said that every night before he went to bed, St Anastasios would curse Plato: 'God, damn Plato!' Then one night, St Anastasios had a dream wherein he met Plato face to face, and he had a chance to speak with him and upbraid him for his errant teachings. When St Anastasios was done with his tirade, Plato responded and said, 'When Christ descended into Hades to preach the Gospel, I was the first to be converted.'

    – Metropolitan Kallistos Ware of Diokleia

TIE AS LEASH

Tie as leash
Child as feral
Home as kennel as sanitorium
This as rehab
Tears as rattling
This as cold turkey
ADHD as *cadaan* bullshit
Radiator as anchor
Ankle as boat
ADHD as bad behaviour
Tie as love.

IN CONVERSATION
WITH SAROD

We talk about how to keep a flame alight
on a charred wick, and the view from my window.

The pitch bends and settles in unfamiliar stations.
I see the rain as if anew from my window

and ask about key changes, he sighs;
there is only sorrow I describe from my window.

So we talk about the candle, scent of sandalwood,
amber, apple and moss are lost from my window.

He says, Samatar, it is we who are the instruments
strummed by our losses that wait by the window.

WE PLAYED SOME OPEN CHORDS

There's something I don't want to do again
– to play my part in a winged victory
for the sullen because I have given this
all that I know of love, which is say
nothing of love and yet the sum total
of everything I've seen of this world
through the eyes of a painter
whose impressions of a French accent
sounded more inflected, like a form
of Italian buried long ago
beneath a volcano, among those that knew
a kiss in the rain (I know, I know),
but a kiss in the rain...

LOOKING FOR FLOWERS
IN WINTER

Tomorrow's the fourteenth, brown branches,
brittle, bare on the blackberry bush.
Buds, not brave enough to break the bark,
if that's what you call it, skin baked in ice.
I was the last to know, being as I was
besotted with how to be; in bloom,
a black bluebell beating to turn towards
the beams, the burning ball; all the buoyancy
in a bathtub, behaviour becoming
a bee looking for beacons in winter,
Black-Eyed Susan, Baby's Breath, Bleeding Heart.

Love, I'm the bird that beatifies this brick
storehouse for a basket of breadcrumbs,
a bed of nails, just to believe, be alive, beloved.

THE EPIC OF CADER IDRIS PLAYLIST

Floating Points – *Promises*
Four Tet – *Rounds*
h hunt – *Playing Piano for Dad*
Brian Green – *Impressions in F Major*
Green House – *Six Songs for Invisible Gardens*
The Vernon Spring – *A Plane Over Woods*
Sam Wilkes – *Wilkes*
Gendel & Wilkes – *Music for Saxofone & Bass*
Duval Timothy – *Sen Am*
Resavoir – *Resavoir*
My Bloody Valentine – *m b v*
Jon Bap – *Let It Happen*
Komachi – *Meitei*
Pharoah Sanders – *Live in Paris (1975)*
Arthur Verocai – *Arthur Verocai*
Pastor T.L. Barrett – *Like a Ship*
Michael White – *The Blessing Song*
Beverly Glenn-Copeland – *Ever New*
Darondo – *Didn't I*
MNDSGN – *Snaxx*
Earl Sweatshirt – *Some Rap Songs*
Nick Drake – *Hanging on a Star*
Bill Evans – *Peace Piece*
House of Lords – *Fanfare for Effective Freedom*
Arthur Russell – *World of Echo*
water feature – *in the world generally*
Fergus McCreadie – *Forest Floor*
Mary Lou Williams – *Black Christ of the Andes*

Sam Gendel – *Rio Nilo 66*
Kendrick Lamar – *Damn*
Arp – *Reading a Wave / Pastoral Symphony / Wild Grass I & II*
John Nash & Suzanne Kraft – *Passive Aggressive*
Pino Palladino & Blake Mills – *Notes with Attachments*
Frank Ocean – *Endless*
Radiohead – *Kid A*
Eliot Smith – *Waltz #1*
Grizzly Bear – *Yellow House*
Beatles – *All You Need Is Love*
Radiohead – *All I Need*
Björk – *All Is Full of Love*
Portished – *Biscuit*
Crosby, Stills & Nash – *Helplessly Hoping*
Tom Algorithm – *Clouds*
John Martyn – *Go Down Easy*
Joy Division – *Love Will Tear Us Apart*
Sam Wilkes & Jacob Mann – *Perform the Compositions of Sam Wilkes & Jacob Mann*
Melissa Aldana – *12 Stars*
Charlie Brown Jr. – *Só os Loucos Sabem*
Big Thief – *Simulation Swarm*
Mary Lou Williams – *Mary Lou Williams*
Orion Sun – *Mango (Freestyle / Process)*
Sven Wunder – *Pentimento*
Radiohead – *Desert Island Disk*
Luke Temple – *Given Our Good Life*
Skullcrusher – *Two Weeks in December*
Fela Kuti – *He Miss Road*
Eric Clapton – *Layla*
Fuubutsushi – *Bolted Orange*
King Krule – *The Ooz*

Yussef Kamaal – *Black Focus*
Toumani Diabaté, Ballaké Sissoko – *Kadiatou*
Pat Thomas – *Gyae Su*
The Chordettes – *They Say It's Wonderful*
The Cure – *Inbetween Days*
Daphni – *Always There*
The Rolling Stones – *You Can't Always Get What You Want*
Blick Bassy – *Wap Do Wap*
Bremer/McCoy – *She's Alive*
Time Wharp – *Spiro World*
caroline – *Dark blue*
XXXTENTACION, Joey Bada$$ – *infinity (888)*
The Fall – *Totally Wired*
The Smashing Pumpkins – *Silverfuck*
Kendrick Lamar – *6.16 in LA*
Kendrick Lamar – *meet the grahams*
Kendrick Lamar – *Euphoria*

THE SNAIL

I mean the analogy writes itself
like the onion in a grand conceit
though we really are like two slugs
in a derelict mausoleum.
Google 'snails are...'
Dangerous. Slow.
Destroying my garden.
Our jobs and our women.

You, who cannot speak snail,
wouldn't understand how the shell
was the gift and curse of diaspora,
how our songs and laments resound
in our half-remembered houses
that we carry to forget, to carry on.

[ETYMOLOGIES]

i. Albion

Albion, as in *Al Bayoon*, the in-between
is all I hear when you glare at me
from across the parapet. *Bayoon*
you and I, this stitch of browning turf
is Albion, soaked and distending.
And *bayoon* the earth and the sky -
auroras that may or may not appear
bayoon our faintly mumbled forfeitures.

Albion, as in purgatory, or perhaps
an oasis, or mirages in the sand,
the cruelest state in limbo;
to think for a moment the in-between
could be anything but Albion,
could be anything but a home.

ii. Gauls

I think of concentric circles, Vercingetorix,
a siege within a siege ad infinitum
until the distinctions between them,
a caesar and a chieftain is reduced
to phases of echoes, phases and epochs
between the wings of moths.

Gaul, somewhere about the guts, stomach
for a fight that can't be won; *kaala kaala;*
as in *gaal* in her motherland;
as in bile, yellow belly, as in coward,
the gall to run around in circles;
and the balls to settle down, here,
this hallowed, hollowed out home
that crept up and swallowed everything.

iii. Iceni

I seen I and I through the mirror
that sits between us like midsummer heat;
almost invisible, like the stencil of words
whispered at the front on a frosty morning.
Some long dead queen rousing her disciples
who for the first time are losing their feet
and the words to prayers; lost in the writing
along the Roman wall.

But I know I cannot see you either.
Not yet, though I will wait a while longer
for you to pull me close enough to witness
to take my bony, phony hand and feel
how frail we have become, captured
by the figments in the glass.

THE PEN

I come from a curious place where the prisoners
are their own wardens. They sleep on time;
rouse themselves in the morning with venom
of staff sergeant smuggling piles
like pikelets. They do all their chores,
break up their owns fights and every now
and then someone stabs himself.

Each prisoner sleeps with a skeleton key
tucked under their pillow. There's a rota
for oiling the locks and every night
they're up in the watch towers –
it's always a code red, a stray
dog triggers a panic and someone,
somewhere, will ask if that was you?

PORTRAIT OF COLOSSUS AS AN IMMIGRANT

I picture him fixed in stride across wandering oceans;
a bridge, reluctant between immovable banks,
wedged like a fallen tree, an angel.
It's a footing that keeps him sentinel and sleepless,
knowing a slip in the east is all it takes
to bring him to his knees, then face-down into Rome.
I want to scale his limbs; sit in the brass of his ear,
whisper on the similitudes of the world. How
at such great heights all language is a blur,
people indistinguishable as fields of corn, sand...
But he's all eyes on the water,
its movement and liberty;
the trick of being everywhere at once.

THE INVADERS

I am parrot's feather, pennywort,
water fern and primrose.
I am the susurrus of grey squirrels
in the branches by your windows.

I carry crayfish plague through fenland
wash and highland stream.
My thick roots tear at the bedrock
under country lane and tower block.

I am a London gang of parakeet;
the coypus close to you as skin.
The sand that beds your cobbled streets,
things will never be the same again.

THE N WORD

Taken out of context, six black letters
on a white page, a word with Latin
                not African roots.

The many Roman synonyms:
taeter, malificus, piceus.

Morum: the black mulberry fruit.
Atratus: clothed in black.

But *nigrum* made its way to us.
Its two syllables a kick and snare.

The front stress a gut punch, low
blow knocking the wind out of you.

A schwa hangs limp behind
like still fruit from the branch

and in that violence
in the midst of all the violence

vowels are choked, 'I' suffocated
even when taken out of context.

STEP THIS WAY

When asked to step this way
you'll fear that the look of not again
will scream guilty, bring out the mugshot
in your babyface; dilated eyes
hauling their weight like a porter:
false testimonies, the betrayal of friends.

Don't resist. Just step their way
into a world of hidden accusations. Engage,
however painful, in their polite interrogations
dressed as small talk   why this flight,
this destination. Ignore the unease of fellow
passengers, the empty seats beside us.

Whatever you do, don't bark
I've stepped your way my whole life;
let's face it, you look the part
black/brown, 5'4" to 6'6", dreadlocks
to balding to bearded to bomb. Please.
Don't be quick with *I'm an Englishman.*

Why should they believe you?
You scarcely believe it yourself.

TURTLE NECK

I've been wearing caps and beanies
like a kippah, a kufi, a shtreimel,
pulled low, my ushanka in the snow,
peak tipped to the moon, my fez
of brittle pride, my scotch bonnet
burning crown, my plumed feathers.
I've been wearing caps and beanies
since a boy, a cloaking adaptation
under shemagh, beret and spodik,
to tuck the eyes behind a shallow
turban; the invisibility of night
        a borrowed dusk.

Know this: I swallow every breath
of air like a turtle playing Russian roulette
with his neck.

HARGEISA

Someone says in passing you see these houses
of corrugated tin, they shrink under the sun
like shrivelled skin and because I have not been
inside a tin house I try to imagine the walls
rippling, rippling, caving in.

Someone says in passing by houses we mean
sheds unfit for tools and shovels, we mean
only paupers and fools would call them houses
I try to imagine the ever-so-faint sizzling, laying
my kids to rest on the stone-baked ground.

Someone says in passing I see myself in
four-poster beds, marble columns, butlers
and maids, twelve-course meals, a raise,
but you see these houses, but you see
these houses, you see these houses.

SEED

i.

My people love like a seed
that doesn't know which way to sprout.
We are always, nearly, bursting.
We keep it together, unsure
what will happen if we breach the testa;
what kind of embryo will dare to venture.

I don't know much about seeds
except that we do our best to hide
the hilum that covers half our skin,
that these days, we are always nearly
laughing and crying.
Always, nearly, at the same time.

ii.

We are losing track of the days
it rains inside the house, outside
we trace footprints in shallow water.
We are losing track of the days.

It rains inside the house, outside
we greet each joke with the last laugh
and home is the air we pass between us.
It rains inside the house, outside.

We trace footprints in shallow water,
always a step behind, a day behind,
but for the amnesia of puddles
we trace footprints in shallow water.

We are losing track of the days,
always a step behind, a day behind.
We are losing track of the days,
and home is the air we keep within us.

SHIELD

If this is the year so be it.
Droughts in places used to rain.
Floods flash unannounced
while every species save our own
clambers for higher ground.
I'm sat on the N63, temple tight
tapping against the window
while a mother wrestles a pram
in the storm – I wonder if she knows
we can't shield them.

>My rains are the most English thing about me.
>Short bursts of drizzle, really quite pathetic,
>like a misty glaze over the eyes: the one before
>the one too many – something like that.

Today, my brother played me *Ave Verum Corpus*
and I wouldn't say his lips quivered but they more than twitched,
I shouldn't have seen it but I did and now I know for sure that
the climate is changing all around me.

And only an hour before I discovered Bill Evans' *Peace Piece*
– the only way my colleagues might have guessed
is if they'd have placed a seismometer on my chest.

                        I can't show them the glue that stitched
                            the montage: the first time I lifted
              her to my eyes, the first time she called me *Abo*
                      and I knew she knew what that meant.

I can't promise this bust-up shield will hold.
That this tattered umbrella can keep what I love
dry, but I promise I'll try.

GOOLE STATION

After Heaney

i.

An absent father's fate is like an oriel
that grew out of the front of a house
and only thinks of the observatory
he can't see, with the grandfather clock
that might be in the shed, though
he conjures it firm in the road ahead
where the sunbeams blush along a row
of diamond trellises that go so well
with the cockcrow in April.

Because a window dreams of wheels
U-turns, knowing the illusion
of the foreground, forward motion,
foresight. Even the moon withdraws
her smile when she's behind you.

ii.

One day, I hope to wriggle myself free
of a certain type of pondering
because I have been imprisoned
by the questions that most men leave
to their children and still
I hope to sit with you in a park
of your choosing, at a time when the sun

sets like the final days of a noble king's
reign, where the proof that gold
is only crystallised light pools around us.
The doves above our heads
sing the hymns of their ancestors
as you ask me what it was
that made the willow weep?

iii.

Gull Lewth, the 'Barn by the Stream',
where the last train from London stopped short.
I waited on the platform in uneasy suppliance
until I heard you'd made it through and relief
carried me away as if the Holy Spirit
designed the moment; poured thatch on the roof;
lit oil lamps, sticks of sage; called a pony
to keep me company under the eastern sky

until the guardians, their shift complete, appeared
as if commanded with coffee, a taxi home,
while the sweet scent of Bethlehem smudged away
the years and all I could think of was Maryam,
a name like the liturgy, for all
who hope for mercy seek to know.

THE GALLOWS

Sometimes I look upon my blessings
like a thief who, recalling his summers,
smiles on the way to the gallows.

THE MUG

The thing with mugs is when they break
even by hairline fracture, they are lost
to purpose, leaking like warm skin,
coffee soaking into tablecloth, wood grain.

No matter how hard you try
to pour yourself inside –
a broken mug is a broken mug
despite the mug's desire

to hold all of what might have been received –
something to plug the cracks
and cover the stains from last year's mess.
A broken mug is a broken mug

and a fool is a fool is a fool
by repetition.

QUASIMODO AND ESMERALDA

Nocturnes. A pot to store the ashes
of barbecues that never went to plan,
incinerated scratch cards, petty-petite
souvenirs nicked from the gift shops
of imagined places, where an outcast
now refuged in the church of our lady,
now Mary now Esmeralda,
each remote as the sacred vase, figured
urn for the dying light of stars,
hung from the pulpit, above our heads,
over crosses, our vacant beds.

LAYLA AND MAJNUN

All that remains of the man is a mound
that meets a mountain, greets afflicted
lovers with that familiar family of wisdom
exclusive to those driven feral, a rabid
branch of epistemology, paradigm
through which to construct a unifying

theorem, love's brittle lens –
how it swallows the stolen light
and it dapples across her body
like a satin dress,
blouse she never asked for
and doesn't know how to return to
our dimmer our duller world
after she's gone.

KALEIDOSCOPE (I)

I will not sleep tonight.
Muezzin is warming up his voice box,
there's a bokeh glow behind the curtains
and this bed-skin is too hot-cold,
my body is last night's microwave meal,
confetti drips from the ceiling
scrambling inner-eye scribbling graffiti
– all the words I can't spell hunt-haunt.
How can you even see them kaleidoscope
symbols that pass through your walls?

If I could love myself I'd be a virgin, pressed olives.
We left it too late and now apologies are grunts
that sound like *haha, aha, ahem, amen*
because at the equator, water doesn't spin swill swirl
down the drain it just drops like my skinny guard.
Kaleidoscope. Kaleidoscope. All I can hear is the aythan
behind the curtains and I can't believe it's not butter.
I can't believe I'm not better, Kaleidoscope.

REQUIEM

To fill the space

                         you

left

                                  with

                                            Echoes

Echoes

                Echoes

                              Echoes

Echoes

                    Echoes

          Echoes

BROKEN BISCUITS

| happy sh@pper |
| magic sponge **dabbed** on a child's grazed knee |
/ *fairy dust* at the bottom of the box /
GUNPOWDER
at the bottom of someone else's barrel:
humpty dumpty putting together a jig/saw with the last {custard cream} *
happy sh@pper * the odd one out \ the last to be picked / still
standing @ back against the wall; *fragile* | **handle with care** / Whoops? *Or do
we spell it* Opps √ BUYER BEWARE # enter at your own risk $ you have been
warned % happy sh@pper % soggy soft ^ someone left the lid off ^ reduced
price ! well past the sell by date \ only sold in foreign shops / only fit for
misfits and other broken biscuits ? the plasters never seem to fit the cut < they
stick to skin >
The things you say you'd do to be whole again.
happy sh@pper
because it's always someone else n e v err you
GRINDING YOUR TEETH
punching an empty wall
no registered GP | dentist | no forwarding addresses |
just pre-existing comorbid codependent & co.
conditions
like coco biscuits with coconuts
someone
licked
the chocolate
off our cookies & put them back
I wish they had just eaten them
happy sh@pper
crabs in a bucket

theyre re: re: re:
always at it
ginger nuts &&& fingers
3 ... 2 .... 1 .... FIGHT!!!
riot over sleights and space
and it's always them   not I   or we
!!! I hate them !!!
more and more
every single time
they remind me

.

MARBLES

What they don't tell you about the kids on the estate
are the marble collections, all the invention
of kids who make a hundred games out of nothing.

Except they're not nothing, are they, these marbles?
In the right hands they can be anything
– eyes for funerary masks; the Elgin Marbles.

Planets in the tiny hands of titans.

And one by one we have them taken from us.
Confiscated in schools,
a safety hazard

– some of us learn to hide them,

or think we've hidden them,
not daring to look inside purses
that haven't been opened in years;

just giving the bag a shake from time to time,
only to find ourselves doubting again
whether the *clack clack* was ever really there at all.

THE HAMMOCK

after Frost

Not quite the silken tent, but a hammock
of woven hemp, sturdy enough to carry us both.
You were never one to panic at the threat
of weather, your careful study of counterbalance,
how each fancy fold of fabric assumes its share
of the load, how the slack and tug of tension
is a sort of Taoist magic, once you surrender
you get the knack of floating.

But if I end up face down
under the weight of expectation
it wasn't for the lack of trying.
I never dreamt of being seated in mid-air
and where I come from, a man can either fly
or fall and floating is for the birds.

حرية

I figure if I keep on in this direction
the path will open the way a crocodile opens.
God can see me nudging forward,
a mouse nibbling on the rind.
I didn't know what to do with myself
– defence for idle hands, like leather
gloves that recall what it felt like
to be skin, to be frost-bitten.

If I smell the slightest hair
of oud I hear Mohamed Abu –
this is why I cannot sleep with ease.
Daydreams of fjords, Björk
plays with my nose,
It is happening, again.
And the many senses reunite
by the fountain, in the white wood.

Sometimes, I don't know the way back
to my house. All it takes is a miscued
shortcut that sends you off like a ricochet
north by north-east to south by south-west
which should be easy to compensate for
except the street looks just like the one
we used to know, don't you remember?
When we lived in the garden?

Homeric. The horses you burn in the fields
in which you lost someone, at a rave
surrounded by the zodiac, a fickle devotee
that kept dancing when your ecstasy

took a manic turn, a search as futile
as the things you tell yourself; that love
is in the weight of webbing,
ta-da, by the pull of a string.

Rhizomic. The way you excavate yourself.
Sift the sand from the stone,
the hand from the bone,
the land from the home
until stripped back to a scout;
the hypha to stretch the furthest
into the bit between or beyond
the outer limit of things.

I fell in love with a fractal.
A voice in a dream I had as a child
that I couldn't know then
belonged to a master hypnotist
— *scares me more now* —
they live in my attic
with all the other moving parts.
Relax Figrao, belíssimo, now breathe.

Liminal. The one who taught me the word,
one morning, on the platform at Waterloo
when the clocks had stopped.
I couldn't love her then. I can't love her now.

Time never applied to us, not here –
the train will never leave the station,
the gloop will neither settle nor flow –
I don't know why I needed it to.

Novalis. It holds the same as clay, keeps
the grain, forests of sunflowers cheat the night
a nebula of luminescent florets,
fireflies swing-lo to the gospels, hymns
that leave no quarter for shadows,
not even a recycled shawl
lifeless along the cobbled way,
not even the memory of it – whatever it was.

I figure if I keep on in this direction
past the mythos and logos, past
the standards of the watchful eye –
a telos will burn as the beacons burn
and all the wasted breaths
that slipped past the open gate
will cheer you on, so long as
you keep on in this direction.

There's a bit that Plato left out
about the lad who escaped the pen,
only to lurch about, hands stretched
out like truth before him. Socrates
found him in his barely audible regret:
If I keep on in this direction
they might still be waiting for me
where it's warmer, by the fire.

Now fight the feeling that a coffin
is the spaceship you desired,
that final triumph of DMT, the smidgen
of dust of you in a volley of Gulf Stream,
a parcel of hues and all the lullabies
you might have shaped into hands
to ease your daughter to sleep
are reaching for you now.

I figure if I keep on in this direction
the path will open like a portal.
The ones we used to know so well,
remember? We lived in a garden
among ageless fruit trees, flowers
like a crowd of cheering faces;
a host of terracotta soldiers
sleeping at our feet.

Platonic. And all that was denied
clogging the sink plug with dead skin –
I've been moulting again, I speak
in cicadas, what is there to deny
when the night beats through us,
through the abdomen, a tymbal
too close to the heart, a friend
to a stranger you once knew well.

Deinosuchus: and his big gob –
big enough to swallow a dual carriageway.
I've seen hardened men hyperventilate
long before the gates were closed.
I've watched them beg to be chained

to radiators, metal bed posts,
grey flames that keep the cell warm,
for someone to pass the time with.

DAFFODILS AND DAISIES

It's the sort of day set in arpeggios.
Played on koras and glockenspiels.
Everyone's like daffodils and daisies,
synced to 'Six Songs for Invisible Gardens',
a cute little PA system in a greenhouse
where the sound is so clear you can hear scales
in the bubbling white noise, a distant fountain;
the odd chirrup and cheep.

And you swell, humbled
because it isn't every day you stop to notice
all this is happening now.

Good Lord wasn't I close? Millimeters,
an atom's length of time, a photon
from the light, for a blink of the eye.

GLISSANDO

i.
Glissando between the bedroom and the stairs,
between the twirling ladders of sleep.
There's a man with names and dialects
born between two slices of bread –
both stale but in different ways –
both mouldy, *could be penicillin*,
but until the crust is broken there's no way to tell.

ii.
Hell must be a state of awareness.
Something akin to Peter reliving his denial,
an endless glissando between a few short sentences
to sum you up like thirty silver pennies
that will jangle in your hands forever.

And the fire will leave you to yourself.

iii.
It's raining in every room, the cat slides
about the marble floor, her tongue curled towards the clouds.

Of all the ways to die, she purrs

                living shouldn't be one of them

reliving shouldn't be one of them

                living shouldn't be one of them

reliving shouldn't be one of them

                living shouldn't be one of them

reliving shouldn't be one of them

                living shouldn't be one of them

reliving shouldn't be one of them

空気を読む

I saw lilies on pond water
I was passing on a train to no place.
I saw lilies still as cadavers.

A wind turbine turns in a frozen field
where once there was only wind.
I watched the wind turn the blade.

Life does this sometimes, sometimes always,
sits like a two-way mirror between us
while the wind tips the balance.

And the lilies are still out there, floating,
waiting for someone to fish them out.
I might have tried but my lungs are blown.

I was passing on a train to no place
through flat, fallow Lincolnshire
where the sky sags low enough to rip

between the blades, harakiri drawn-out
feudal punishment, while the last of us
are breathing the last of it through straws.

THE UNIVERSE FORMERLY
KNOWN AS GOD

mad Nietzsche pissing himself
frantic in purgatory's psychiatric ward
galloping, the laughing horseman
they'll never get it in High German
abyss abyss in Low Latin

sedated Nietzsche flits between livid
and despondent and begs the Universe
to stop with the jokes, *enough*
he cries, *I've had enough of the abyss ...
those flaxen eyes ... those tawny flames ...*

ORPHEUS AS A BUSKER

He doesn't do it for spare change lobbed into his lap;
he plays to regain the power to halt coins in mid-air
like back in the day when his lyre could outdo Sirens.
He doesn't do it for small talk or drunken sing-alongs;
he strums away assured of his comeback, certain
that he'll be found in a mixolydian sludge of notes,
food for the muses. He plays on a prayer that Zeus
will reappear and end the moratorium on magic,
that one day this marginal busker, armed with his music
will repair the disenchantment, make us all believe again.

THE GAME

I'm running in a quantum field
through dense hay, climbing bales
of warm static stacked like Intihuatana
        to rest and get my bearings.
It's like being in one of those 8-bit worlds,
where you can almost see the integers,
the lines of code that keep you.

It made me question is life a game?
A VR-enhanced MMO, the full life-like
        smell of Chanel on her lapel;
goosebumps that read like braille,
lips that really bruise, in all worlds,
though this is more Space Invaders at the arcade,
eight points on a joystick, the dharmachakra,
where the magic is in the limitations,
the building blocks you can't quite fashion
but fathom nonetheless.

You'll hear singing bowls and hand gongs serene
but even at this level you won't know where it's coming from.
Strings set their wicks alight, set like bosons
eclipsing bosons. It all looks so familiar

take it all in

game over

respawn

run along.

ORISONS

There's no I in us or them
or we.
Hence the Sufi
sips from the flagon
but keeps balance
like a trapeze artist
offsetting the lilt
against the tilt
of a globe unsteady
on its axis.

> *In the old poetics*
> *there was no 4th wall to break*
> *You were the chorus*
> *participant*
> *& God was in the audience.*

This is how they made
music for plants;
orisons read into seawater
to make it sweet again.
And all the children lived
for a thousand years.

Rumi's ruin, the suicidal wishes
of a sage, to be submerged,
to drown in nectar, subsumed
in honey, a firefly in amber,
makes me wonder, there's a fine line
between the strait path and straight jacket;
a thin lattice splits the confessional,
and all the saints
                    in this house
are stumbling
into heaven   hell
and   dying
with their   beards
black.

BRENIN LLWYD

There must be a Celtic word
for when the clouds droop and drape
along the munros' spires, diffuse enough
to shift shape, now a harras of horses
concealing their grey king like a dagger
tatty in the sleeves of fog

Perhaps an expression fit for the one
stood in the glen below, who lost a hand
and an eye in last year's mist, who
just can't get the boggy stench of time
out of their noses, locked
in the peatland's pores. Go on,
tell yourself it's just a pile of stone,
the sky a hoax in the light...

Tell yourself this is another sonnet
about hills and ponies in the atmosphere,
its author a fool who stole the chords
off a ghost who saw the Angels of Mons,
who knows that neither should be here,
dressed up as some brave mountaineer,
when the count's off and it's all performing,
and he shits himself in the morning.

Leave him to his myths and delusions,
to the drayage between worlds when he says
the tears of a single bristlecone hedge
could flood the lowlands to the skies,
until the dew sits over the oceans
and all that is living, and already dead,

sink into the darker light.

ON THE END OF THE WORLD

after Czeslaw Milosz

Nothing is out of the ordinary.
Burnt toast softens with a foil-scrape of butter.
Lukewarm cupper, builder's,
teased with futile drip-drip of milk dregs.
The shower, much like the weather, indecisive,
fluxing between too cold and scolding.
The sky an old English off-white,
deathbed sheets of a fever patient.
Nothing is misplaced. Books and coffee mugs
cover the kitchen surface, a kettle whistles,
taking its place among the tired motifs
of any old morning; the wooden steps
tapped by her unhurried feet, her footstep arias –
each creak and groan of old pine staccato
tells me she's not running   falling   screaming.
We pass with mumbled greetings.
She hovers at the sink, runs water through fingers
into the glass, brings it to eye level.
Looks at the sun through its prism,
orange pulled apart in water.
Haven't you heard? The Sun has exploded,
in 8 minutes the world will end.

She points to the radio, so
I turn it on. It's Beethoven –
not the Moonlight Sonata, or the 5th,
but the Eroica; not the funeral march
but the scherzo. She points to her glass
like a conductor's cue before the ictus.
I peep behind the curtains; half-asleep children
climb onto school buses, miss their parents' waving;
a cat climbs a fence. 4 minutes. Your toast'll go cold.
I pause before charred slabs, turn and catch
the cat's eyes, find in its golden light a likeness,
fix in the metronome of its blinking –
light on, light off, light on, light off.
She looks at her watch. Hurry,
you'll be late for work. I dress in half-light,
fetch sandwiches from the fridge,
check the time, kiss her forehead, sip her water.
Bye love! Grab my wallet, my keys.
Step into the street and almost miss the cats
now gathered in litters on the lawn.
Songbirds chirping madly.
Labradors and terriers staring at the sky.

THE END OF HISTORY

I had for many years forgotten the night
the Greatest Circus in the World
performed its greatest trick,
packing itself away into mucky crates
and disappearing before dawn.

Tonight, all I can remember is that circus
as I watch our country fold into folds
like a scrunched-up map
and wonder about that old trick,
the sleight of hand, the puff of smoke.

A DARKER LIGHT

There is much to be said about moths.
– how a caterpillar feeds on its own flesh,
and the trust it takes to eat yourself
uncertain of the resurrection. Imagine
a caterpillar when it sees the brown
spotted wings of an angel, ascension
of dead siblings risen, lifting
their second lives towards a paradise
that from the caterpillars' vantage
is a visible, flickering Valhalla.
It flinches me that the worms
have no idea what awaits them.

I wonder if it's because cannibals
consume their mother tongues, forget

their past lives, the blind faith
of that gruesome womb.
There is much to be said about a moth
who, in the absence of memory, floats
instinctively towards the nearest heaven
and I want to call it a neon heaven
but that would limit the signal
to fraudulence – omit the danger.
There is much to be said about the intention
to circumambulate at the first sign of fire,
again and again, a distorted ritual, gnarling
all that was beautiful, those injured wings

until, one by one, these angels fall
and still, there is much to be said of it all.

SLIPSTREAM

I saw a roadkill bird (a raven-like thing)
sewn into the highway, it was hard to tell
body from tarmac save a plumed limb
that must have escaped the wheel.
I watched that feathered bough flip and flap
every time a car passed,
which was often on this stretch of road.
I watched it for hours. Unable to move.
I see this fledgling spirit in my sleep.
I see it everywhere, even in your eyes
where my reflection used to be.
I didn't ask myself if this is how the dead fly
or ponder the irony.
Only how this, of all analogies,
covers my world in ashes.

Never ask a ghost how it happened.
Most of us are sure we're still alive.

CODA

> The signal is given for Rafā'īl
> to draw a cold breath, lips pursed
> on the brass mouth of a horn
> that spans the glacial width
> of measurement itself
> – we brace ourselves, for a note
> that will cut through the air
> like shrapnel, a signal to roll back
> the black rug of the world.

There's a loop between the foetal shell
 and these fists that feign a foreign brand
of defiance like the songs the sailors know
when they're coming into port in Sevastopol
– there's sawdust in the bread and water –
takes you back to Osowiec, where the dead
are gaining yards and real estate.

Boys, we must resign ourselves to oblivion
to depart from the fear that attaches
to our fibres like cigar smoke.
It's the only way to smother the hope
of anything other than mortars over chlorine
bullets over shrapnel, one in the heart
over one in the eye, frostbite over gangrene,
mice over rats, retreat over advance,
and anything over a fresh offensive.

A white boy calls me to Ypres.
He has waited, this boy of seventeen,
waited while the long line of boys
has barely budged in a hundred years.
He does not wait with them
but for one of his own to conduit
the taste of iron and innocence
mixed with scattered salt
– he can't get the acid off his tongue
while he searches for lemon trees
on these fields of ritual sacrifice.
Son of my grandson, he says,

you will feel the moment
the gates are closing
by the muffling of the ears
and distance.

And some of us can sense
a tension in the ribbons that bind us,
a weariness in the paragons
that bring our infants to laughter,
while the imperceptible movement
of the small hand ticks along.
And some of us are resigned
that nothing good can come
from that deathly pitch
or our deadly silence.

THE ALGORIDDIM

thinks I'm all about half-arsed poems and brutal cage fights.
My biggest issue here is that I opened this half-arsed poem
with "The Algorithm / thinks ..."

But it knows (of course it doesn't know)
but somehow it does, no? Knows
that I know it knows and so
as crazy as this sounds I'm sure
it predicted or perhaps pre-empted
this half-arsed poem

and suggested this terrifying deep fake
titled UFC greatest hits
Al Gore waltzing towards me
to the tune of the Imperial March
pulls out a Nokia 3210, flashlight
becoming lightsabre, the ref
too busy swiping right to see
the snake
running rings
all around us.

DO YOU HAVE YOUR DUNNY DOCUMENTS FOR ARMAGEDDON?

I had been waiting for the sky to fall
for the last ear of corn to make front page
or something of the sun to fry the wiring
sending us back before the freezing,
when out of nowhere, the fifth horseman –
came riding on the back of an Andrex puppy
and everyone went potty for bog roll.

Nothing will ever shit me up more
than seeing Aunty Layla tear lumps out of Craig
with the dodgy knees from two doors down,
for the last bag of crap wrappers cos everyone knows
there are no dartboards at the apocalypse,
no bullseyes, no holes-in-one – just cortisol turds
plastering the sides like a dodgy plumber
caught in that messy liminality
between states of matter.

England. Let that be the last secret between us.
Don't despair, there's a factory in Wapping
churning out reems of shit tickets.
We don't have to walk alone...
So in this renewed spirit,
let us share what paper we have,
take these Rizlas, and pinch
a little pinch of imagination.
I'll be the first to let it go, after all,
there's always enough water under the bridge.

A PALE BLUE FLOWER

grows out of the asphalt.
A single bud and leaf held together
by a tiny bit of green.

>   If you knew what it was like
>   to be laid so still you'd notice
>   when the ground takes the air
>   the trees exhale.

This year was too much wasn't it?
I mean it wasn't just me was it?

A pale blue flower, dry and bony.
There are ten rooms stacked
on top of ten more rooms
and every one of them lonely.

> *I didn't want to be an artist*
> *But Gia reads me her eulogy*
> *I can't think what else to do with it.*

>   Laid is a funny word.
>   Because of where I come from
>   I pronounce it lied

while a hikikomori in the first room
counts the number of times
his mind goes blank.
54, 55, 55, 55, 58...

> She says *I knew you gonna be
> a troublesome child* but I nursed you
> as if you were my own.

> But because of where I come from
> when I think of laid
> I think of carcasses sealed and lyed
> stacked ten to a barrel
> and I vow never to drink milk again.

THE EPIC OF CADAIR IDRIS
(RHIZOMATIC MEDITATIONS)

*

(appassionato: sfz)

When I find you,
will you know what it was that brought me to this mountain?
A painful fruit once devoured.
The sharp edges of its seeds lodged
like a whooping cough
that would neither flower nor wither.

What is the soul if not a walled garden?
I tell myself I carry Isfahan between my shoulders.
Look into my eyes and see wild orchids;
pomegranates the size of melons;
mangoes the size of raisins.

Idris, your name is older than the fall of Babel.
In the deserts we speak your name.
Peace be upon you.
And recall our earliest memories
when we gazed up the never-ending bodies
of our fathers, to imagine you standing before us.
We write in the manner of your teaching
and place the word on the highest pedestal.

Here, at the head of the chair,
I accept your challenge.

*

(4/4: 90 bpm: f)

Poetry – I know I'm given to foolery.
Always had a death wish I'm living my eulogy.
Always soon to be but never making it,
never do for the sake of it.
Aint from around here, so when I mispronounce it parquet,
you parrot my teachers
while I focus on the colours in the alphabet.
And when I hold a clarinet, it burns like the cigarette I play.
Beneath the minaret I pray.
I tete-a-tete with the bird of prey circling my people
while I plume my feathers.
I'm the hillside moss and heathers;
four seasons, all weathers.
The crowd measures, they feel my temperature,
they see the calm exterior but sense my reservoir.
A lot of the time they don't fully know what I'm on
but we connect at the molecular.
We're clinging to this rock like the breath in a pensioner
and we all sense the blue moon tide.
We feel the gloom inside.
It's our human side.
More times, it's like the captain jumped ship
and the crewmen died.
So I walk with my shoes untied
with the cooked and fried
in my cut and sewn
til the cows come home.

*

(mp)

There were corners that had to be cut.
Unless you wanna overload the circuit, kaput.
And the pieces that you're left with
are the hardy bits that wouldn't give.

A cough can quaff an avalanche
and if I'd have tried to lift a branch
before my back was set
what would've been the sobriquet?

Other than dickhead.
I already cancelled myself for being shit.
Late bloomer, something of a sourdough.
Toxic, where did all the power go?
Didn't I ask you to mind the circuit?

Could have been on another level,
from the heart, nothing special
but I just can't get this hat to sit right.

Feels like a New Era but I can't see up.
Feel worse than a mosque eater,
than a rabbit on Easter.

What would've been the sobriquet?
A noet? A know it all?

Noetry, noetic to some and rust
on a new blade to those who smell
their wines first.

I probably should have left it there
but there's always some botched herbal remedy
promising to get the rust off. So,

you scrub as if the feds are drumming
the door. Your life flashing before…
Splashing the crystal blue water
at a nudist beach.

And we could take it to Siggy and his student,
but what good's that now?
You mad bastard!

If I could show you what I see
projected in inkblots,
in cakes and carpets,
maybe we'd hold hands
or maybe see the funny side,
or maybe.

It's peak. Glue. Nutmeg zoot –
at least we recycle the ashtrays.
Stargaze in the wrong direction
we must be finding our ways.

*

(cresc)

Could this be a tale of the tribe, a re
vison? The incision below the cataracts,
one long swing of the battle axe
through these artifacts of inheritance

that attracts and attacks in tandem.
Could this be a call to the mandem?
I drop pseudorandom vignettes
high on super phantom twinjets.
Musk in the air but who's burning the incense?
Can't believe I thought spiders were insects –
should'av checked the index.
All my life I've been drowning though
the limbs of this poem might be inlets.
The sea is the black that's been flowing out of inkjets.
Take me back to Lismore.
That was how it should have been, visiting Hargeisa.
One long swing with a laser.

I met an Al Somali in Jeddah,
another in Minnesota
and we were all the same –
intermezzo, in medias res,
interluded, amidst
and Albion is everywhere
and nowhere
all the time
never and now.

*

(funebre)

What is the soul if not a haunted place?
A dark parlour.
The via negativa of spirit as void
made a coffin of the anima.
So where do we get the stamina?

To push a boulder up a hill.
To fail and fail again at failing with grace.
My cigarette pops with delight.
Each one a succession of false endings.

Covenants marked in the sands at low tide.
The water is our witness.
I don't think I'm gonna make it this time.
I don't think I'm gonna make it this time.
Oceans rise and I can't see the tide for the horizon.
As I couldn't see the truth through the lies and…
We used to play hide or see
but nobody's finding.
This aint like chumps bidding time
I was frontlinin'
wars that defy describin'
who's ridin'?
We were better as a caterpillar.
Blessed is thee who is the outsider.
Cursed is thee who is the outsider.

I roll the space between us like a Rizla
that's how I see the past, present and future.
Sipping mint tea in Andalusia
hanging from a tree behind Piccadilly Circus
am I nervous? Of course we are.
I lose months of the year to the fear.
None of us are safe here.
First they came for,
next they came for,
then they came for,
when they came for,

no one here for.

I don't think we're gonna make it this time.
I don't think we're gonna make it this time.
Blessed is thee who is the outsider.
Cursed is thee who is the outsider.

*

(sostenuto)

I put up my tent on a gravelly slope
The wind split along both sides
and watched the last of light drain
from the sky, the horizon in this analogy
an exit wound.
People shouted as I climbed.
*You're wasting your time
you're already both mad and a poet.*
But, you see, the challenge said you'd wake up either.

That night was so dark
I was getting closed-eye hallucinations.
I could see really far, as far as Mousa's broch,
which up until recently I thought was a constellation
which is odd cos it also sounds like Mousa's book
and before you know it – *swing lo sweet chariot.*
I prayed for revolution cosy at the Marriot.
Proletariat Iscariot. Watch me bend the knee
for one day as a Poet Laureate.
I looked over the Gwynedd, and what did I see
tell 'em about the nightmare, Samatar...
And I'm doing that thing I hate

I mean it got me this far,
but no, I'm doing that thing again
because I can't get this hat to sit right.

(cresc)

Feels like a New Era but it's all mashed up.
Must be a knock-off.
He must be a fraud.
He must be afraid.
No hair left to braid.
There's rust on my blade.
No hair left to fade.
Scrubbing like the feds are at the door on a raid.
No bud left to grade.
No cards left to trade.
A spade for my suit.
There's sand in my zoot,
my coat and my boot.
Fuck me it's windy up here.

A landslide comes after the rain
but I'll stand in the showers again and again.

*

(4/4: 90 bpm: ff)

My life is Charlie Chaplin, Alfred Hitchcock.
Pitched up at the campsite with a pitchfork.
Punchline the punch drunk and it's lightwork.
I write Kraftwerk and slow jam and post-hardcore
lyrics on a billboard.
Spread lilacs over bloody floorboards.

Keep up with these images.
My life is running two dozen movies in one-screen cinemas.
This is not the thing you think it is.

I saw a man made of brass but all I saw were privileges.
Another made of gold and all that he could hold
in his mittens were carcinogens.

Nutty professors and Nitty Socrates
astronauts shipwrecked in the lunar seas.
I write lunacy into symphonies.
Decode James Joyce Ulysses.
My life is part-Penderecki
part-Achilles but I'm all heels –
blisters on my feet I gotta wait until my soul heals.

They say those who can't listen must feel.
That's why I sliced my off ears in sunflower fields.
My eyes are like five-thousand-horsepower wheels.
My words are a window past a wallflower's shields.

*

(dim)

She invades my thoughts like the man
who makes his living waving a pocket watch
in front of overconfident victims
who labour under the false assurance
that they won't be taken quite so easily
– after they're turned into frogs and chickens
– after they've emptied their pockets
– after their friends have posted it all on TikTok.

And I say
I don't mean
what I say
it just comes out
like fireworks
on New Year's Day
and you say
you don't mean
what you say
it just comes out
like fireworks
on New Year's Day.

*

(solenne)

It's a mystery
how you teleport
telegram, you're in the teleframe
we're stuck together, cellophane,
what's your name again?
There's a body in the boot
You've been digging up skeletons.
I'm in the Skeltons weighing up
pastries, weighing up the bones.
This one was a serial killer
blood pouring out of corn flakes
and this one was innocent.

*

(più mosso)

I should have stayed down in the valley.
Cos the winds on a mazzaleen.
But the skies looking dazzaleen.
Atomic number 53 iodine
lots of dopamine, gasoline.
I know if I could see myself
I'd be shouting happy Halloween.
There was never any in-between.
Flickering through the colours
like the lamp and the kerosene.
If I'd had known what ADHD can do
I would have sold my television.
And maybe chilled out a bit.
Or not as much.
I was never stressed.
Now I feel the pressure.
This poem better be clutch.
And if I do my job right there's a lot of catch
…like Covid-20.
But I'm doing that thing I hate.
Thinking you're banking time not knowing it's a Ponzi scheme.
A click of the fingers and you're back in the room.
You're like "who left this mess, am I in a dream"?
It'll happen again you can only assume.

*

(con fuoco)

I gave the wicker man a struck match
tucked it in his rattan seagrass hat.
He danced, it was the First of May

and the clouds were smoked havanas
and the crowds were chanting my name.
I don't know what it was; bananas...
they couldn't see the crown on my head
weaves of water hyacinth and bamboo thatch.

*

(rfz)

What is the soul if not a diffuser?
A scented humidifier, aroma
like chameleon scales.
I smell it every time the cabin jerks
acute angles and it's a wonder we're still airborne
– it could also be serotonin syndrome
because my eyeballs are sweating
every time I yawn
when I'm thinking about dying –
one eye on the aircrew
cos if they start we're done for –
and one eye scanning the rows
just to make sure that stench
isn't coming from me.

What is the soul if not an altimeter
that soars, clipped to wings
to the chests of photons
that form newly-made haloes for saints
measure the pressure of ascension
accurate to the bar, in all its homonyms.
What is the soul if not an echo sounder
when that's all you have to see

in the dark, the resonance
of someone clearing their throat:
What is this place?
Is anybody here?

*

That message aint getting opened.
That email can get fucked.
Same goes for the other 9999 –
cos the webmail stopped counting.
In fact, let me hide the phone.
I fancy a burger, Wagyu and Angus.
Cheese as thick as sheep.
Shitload of mayonnaise
and a bag of sauce.
All different kinds of sauce.
Smooth chilli sauce, chilli sauce with flakes.
Chilli sauce with chopped chilli,
mix-it-with-more-mayonnaise-if-the-chilli's-too-hot chilli.
Iceberg lettuce and jalapeño chilli.

*

(cresc con autocoscienza)

Into my third set of 18s
Pretty formal poet really, I need structure
but couldn't hold it an arm's length away.
All the shit you can't delay
getting older by the day,
word play will only get me part the way.
I need action

camera
lights.
We are naked under satellites.
Our birth marks and cellulite
til we read our last rites.

And the sunrise, if you can call it that,
a Zippo struggling to spark the clouds
I'm thinking.
thinking did I even fall asleep?
I'm thinking.
thinking I doubt I'll get a poem out of this.
But thinking all the same.

Maybe you have to have slept
for Idris to see you.
In lieu of a change
that dazzling epiphany
I figured I must be neither

a madman

                          nor a poet

                                                just halfway up a hill

hatless,

                        feet on the atlas,

Goodbye Idris

                how about we call it a night?

*

(smz)

What is a poem if not the soul of a man cast before him
either as an eight-sided die – a skimming stone –
or one of the old nets set adrift
in the Sea of Galilee where the fish
are unlike any other fish in the world.

WHERE THE COLOUR BLUE WAS MADE

You will not remember in the morning
so write it down until the nib cuts the paper
        or breaks the skin
if you hurried it on your hands.

Next time the walls bend out of shape
or the stuff in the room begins to vibrate
remember this too will pass.

The Earth shall be green as it once was
and the ocean as if this was where
the colour blue was made.

KALEIDOSCOPE (II) (36MG)

It took as long as it did
to bring me to where the words
in their joined-up handwriting
was yarn for the weft on a weaving loom.

A lifetime under the clouds
– it rained this precious ink
that I dammed for the harvest

but if it never rains again –
I'll be damned if I miss
the piss that falls from the sky,

Verily, I choose thee,
this drought by slow-release

dopamine

– as for the price I might have paid
spare me the prizes

in fancy cloth and linen.
I'm done with all the spinning.

HOW I LEARNED TO FIGHT

like a chewed-up tapeloop
stammering into saw waves –
if you blink really fast you'll see
four quavers and a crotchet
swinging like two ballet dancers
(who learned how to fly
living with the Maasai)
pretending to be water.

ENGLAND

In lieu of a detailed taxonomy,
the names of trees I camped beside;
in lieu of a firm footing,
the solemn recognition

that I know you
more than everywhere else
put together.

Not quite belonging, but
the closest I will come
to finding my home
is walking alone at night's filtered end

over Parliament Bridge
past Nelson's column
up to Camden

up and up
until Hampstead
where the first impressions of dawn
are the songs of birds

whose names
I never had to learn
for them to sing for me.

OHMS

He said *you'll meet but 20 people in a lifetime*.
I take my aphorisms like a dessert, a treat
from a foreigner's delicatessen made familiar
by its sugared coating, the jammy core.

Ours are footprints into a future folklore.
The people of glass and glaciers, glint
screening the glib and gob
of our gentleman's gammy rapport.

Those who look for seashells will find them
knocking against the pearly white cliffs of Dover.
There's a thin line between *barely* and *nearly*
but the kingdom of heaven is taking reservations.

England, to me, is Ohm's law.
Resistance to the flow, the current
trend, the tide of things through circuits:
Tiger Bay by way of Notting Hill ... Toxteth ...

Ohm's law, to me, too close to bone,
round the back of Whitehall carved into stone
that built the centerground; laws
to loosen our concentration,

such that when he said *you'll become 20 people
in a lifetime*, I was barely in the room,
nose in a 99 cone; oi ... *Sam ... Elmi ... Mr. Ahmed ...
Samatar ... ina Daud ... ya Hajji ... Sayiddii ... Abd'Allah*

In the end it was death, the mere mention of it,
he said *you can die well even in a palace.*
So I removed my final mask, took up the only chair that will
have me, nibbled the last slice of cake…

LIGHTHOUSE

for Dorothea Smartt

i.
Every year, I return to a poem that would not be written.
I thought it was a matter of weighing

                      each

                                word

                                        out

that somehow the old bulb in the lighthouse
would flicker ever so slightly,

                      pause

                              Voila!

Folk-sailor-phantoms rising to their post.
The sky heavy with the hatching of moths.

It was simply a matter of waiting.

ii.
Light fell in shafts,
planks of 3 by 4 slatting diagonally.
I'm transfixed by the one that lands at your feet,
the entropy of dust, matted and entangled.

There's no place darker than a closed mouth.
It's November, a breeze
as light as small talk is all
we have left to speak for us.

So I sip sunlight from blackberries
stubborn to the bramble bush
like a leaf in December
that will not fall.

iii.
If at some point I find myself doing the work of a piano tuner,
tightening and loosening the strings by ear,
waiting for harmonics to slip into place
like tectonic plates after disturbance,
or a watchful neglect,
I will cling to your guiding light
as if it were rope. I will labour there
until each note finds its place across the octaves
and the chords we play sustain.

iv.
I prefer nightrise and sunfall,
such that *lightweight*, measures the cargo
of dawn padding down the darkness
to a thin wafer of night on the pavement.
>*Squash it down until it resents itself*
>*its envies and temperature.*

The super-compressed thatch and knitting
of strings that ring out like an upright base
standing idle in the lounge
when all it takes is a cough or a sneeze
to start a conversation, confession,
resurrection, the ascension of nightrise.
>*Bless me doctor for I have sinned,*
>*it's been years since my last confession.*
>*The sun has shrivelled*
>*and I've become accustomed*
>*to a shortening of the light.*

DIE WELT

'Die Welt ist alles, was der Fall ist.'
– Ludwig Wittgenstein

i. I never knew that candlelight
was enough to heat a room,
and so here in this tomb,
I am returned to all the words
ever written about the fires we tame;
that once in a while, briefly,
we dial our compass north
to know the rapture's warmth.

ii. I never knew how pilgrims mourn their losses;
at first, the loss of innocence, shortly after,
time, then the time spent mourning,
though the hardest losses to mourn
are those moments of reprieve,
when you reach beyond the world
for lightness,
a light,
or a lighter,
when anything will do.

iii. For months I dread the fast.
For days I mourn its passing.
Die Welt ist alles, except it's not,
except it is, except it's not, is it?

iv. It just came out.
I was somewhere between
my living room and a k-hole,
between Eliot and Walcott,
a sort of neo-something-or-other,
my socks were pissing wet,
God knows why
only God knows.

v. *Thus whereof one cannot speak*
why must we be vehement?

vi. I heard it said in Akureyri
Dagarnir eru langir

   there are hymns in the bending
   of a leaf towards the moon

   I used to lay with my head
   in the lap of a mound

   Half-dead on the grass
   too much too soon

   the laying of hands
   light through clouds.

ONLY FOALS AND HORSES

Are you really the foal that brought
jump ropes to the stables
and tried to get the whole knacker yard
skipping like kangaroos?
                It was a circus wasn't it, a proper abattoir

But really, are you the foal
who brought jump leads to the morgue
and put the village medium
out of business?
                Every ten-bob Lazarus swears by you

If it is really you let's clamber
to where the water meets the air
where only foals and horses
dare

to reach a hand into the clouds
while we dangle the rest
of our equipment
and wait.

THE KITE

Not today, as soon as the time is right,
or our knees buckle beneath our grudges,
I'll find a clearing in the field where hallows
prayed the penance of falconers.

I'll let out the line and send a kite
up the lowest heaven; a prayer for bridges
to lift me by the grubby tallows
to glimpse the mother's face, to imagine her

lenient, emeritus; citrus peel
falling like scales from eyes now lowered
beneath the clouds only to find a garden
on the edge of town, *something of the ideal
I failed to grasp*; children at the bridle
point, rays of light, the kite turning starboard.

Notes

1. Cader Idris: Nestled within the picturesque Welsh landscape, the formidable Cadair Idris, or "Chair of Idris", is a mountain steeped in legend. It opens a gateway into a realm where myth and reality seamlessly intertwine. Within the annals of time, Idris, an ancient giant king of Northern Wales, emerges as a central figure, making this mountain his throne. The parallels between this Welsh giant king and the Biblical Idris (also described as a giant) deepen with their shared interest in the written and poetic word. It is said that the Welsh Idris issued a remarkable proposition to his subjects, which would forever etch the mountain's name into the collective consciousness: anyone brave enough to spend a single night alone at the summit would, on waking in the morning, either be cursed with insanity or blessed with poetic inspiration. This enigmatic challenge cast an enchanting spell upon the very stones and slopes of Cadair Idris, turning it into a crossroads of destiny.

2. Cadaan: White (Somali) | Abo: Father (Somali)

3. The Invaders: This poem was written in response to the words of MP John Townend (former Tory Scumbag), who said, "England must be reconquered for the English. They should go back from whence they came" (*Guardian*, 29 August 1989).

4. حرية: Freedom (Arabic)

5. 空気を読む: Kuuki o Yomu: "understanding the situation without words" or "sensing someone's feelings" is a very important concept in Japanese culture. The literal meaning is "reading the air". (*BBC*, 30 January 2020; Tokhimo, 7 June 2022).

6. Die Welt: Section V is a line from Wittgenstein's *Tractatus Logico-Philosophicus*, published in 1922. In Section VI, *Dagarnir eru langir* is a lyric from 'Flugufrelsarinn' by Sigur Rós.

7. The first epigraph is from Plato's *Republic*.

8. The second epigraph is a translation from the Greek of words spoken by Metropolitan Kallistos Ware of Diokleia during a talk entitled 'Athens and Jerusalem: Hellenic Paideia and the Greek Fathers.' The passage was reposted, in English and in Greek, on *Logismoi*, the blog of Aaron Taylor, a Russian Orthodox deacon, in 2010.

Acknowledgements

To my family, especially my children: I love you in excess of all measurement and far beyond the reach of poetry. I love you, hooyo, abo, ayeeyo and all my walaalayaal.

#FreePalestine
#FreeCongo
#KeepEyesOnSudan
#HelpForHaiti
#Somalia
#FreeYemen
#StopTheGenocide
#Justice4IssaSeed
#Justice4AdelYussuf
#Justice4DanielMensah

We pray for the end of neocolonialism and justice for all.

بسم الله الرحمن الرحيم

Portrait of Colossus, flipped eye, 2021:
– 'Portrait of Colossus as an Immigrant'
– 'England'
– 'The Invaders'
– 'NIGGER'
– 'Step This Way'
– 'Marbles'
– 'Orpheus as a Busker'

Poetry Review, 2021: 'The Snail'
– Winner of the 2021 Geoffrey Dearmer Prize

More Fiya: A New Collection of Black British Poetry (edited by Kayo Chingonyi), Canongate, 2022:
– '[Etymologies]'
– 'Coda'

'The Epic of Cader Idris (Rhizomatic Meditations)', 2023
– Filmed and recorded under commission by Hull City Arts and Hull Jazz Festival / Out of the Box
– Published in print by *Scarf*

Poetry Wales, 2024: 'Do You Have Your Dunny Documents for Armageddon?'

Prairie Schooner, 2024: 'Ban No Kukki Wo Yomu'

A Note on the Author

Winner of the 2021 Geoffrey Dearmer Prize, Samatar Elmi is an Obsidian Fellow and associate poetry editor at flipped eye publishing. His poems have appeared in *Poetry Review*, *Poetry Wales*, *Prairie Schooner*, *Magma* and *Iota*, and have been anthologised in *More Fiya*, *Filigree*, *After Plath* and *The Echoing Gallery*. Elmi's *Portrait of Colossus* was selected as a PBS Pamphlet Choice, and in 2022 he was commended in the Guardian poetry roundup as a poet whose 'whose plangent lyrics disguise a sharp bite'. As Knomad Spock, his most recent album, *Winter of Discontent*, was critically acclaimed in print (*Clash Magazine*, *Afropunk*, *GoldFlakePaint*, *Eqate Magazine*) and radio (BBC 6 Music, BBC Wales, Amazing Radio, Radio X). Elmi has performed live in session for Janice Long (BBC Wales), at the Aldeburgh Poetry Festival and for the Poetry Society, and he was highlighted as 'One To Watch' at Latitude Festival. He also appeared on BBC Radio 4's 'Warsan Shire on a Nation of Poets'. *The Epic of Cader Idris* has been published jointly by Bloomsbury and flipped eye. *A Darker Light*, Knomad Spock's second album, has just been released.

samatarelmi.co.uk

A Note on the Type

Warnock is a serif typeface designed by Robert Slimbach. The design features sharp, wedge-shaped serifs. The typeface is named after John Warnock, one of the co-founders of Adobe. John Warnock's son, Chris Warnock, requested that Slimbach design the typeface as a tribute to his father in 1997. It was later released as a commercial font by Adobe in 2000 under the name Warnock Pro.

MORE FROM BLOOMSBURY POETRY

If you enjoyed *The Epic of Cader Idris*,
you might like *Sonnets for Albert*
by Anthony Joseph:

LIGHT

Light, fill the air around these houses.
May my grandmother continue to water her roses
and touch the aloe fronds in her forever time.
Light, as you lit the morning my father arrived
unexpectedly in his new Hillman Hunter,
and Mammy ran into the yard to embrace him.
And until my grandfather put wire around the veranda

I could sit and swing my legs off the banister,
or from the garden spy up the thighs of my father's
new girlfriend, as she laughed with ankles crossed,
as Albert moulded his mother's anthuriums.
My grandmother fried fish, we ate, she was happy,
even as she knew that later that afternoon
my father would be gone again into that gone momentum.